# GO, GO, CONSTRUCTION TRUCKS!

## A FIRST BOOK OF TRUCKS FOR TODDLERS

**BONNIE RICKNER JENSEN**

ROCKRIDGE PRESS

Series Designer: Angela Navarra
Interior and Cover Designer: Angela Navarra
Art Producer: Michael Hardgrove
Editor: Laura Bryn Sisson
Production Editor: Nora Milman

Photography: Shutterstock: p. 1, 4, 5, 6, 7, 8, 9, 10, 11, 12, 13, 14, 15, 16, 17, 18, 19, 20, 21, 22, 24, 25, 26, 27, 28, 29, 38, 39, 42, 44, 45, 46, 47, back cover. istock: Cover, 23, 30, 31, 32, 33, 34, 35, 36, 37, 40, 41, 43.
Author Photo: © 2020 Angela Rose Jensen

ISBN: Print 978-1-64739-265-9 | eBook 978-1-64739-266-6
R0

To my dad, Alvin, and my brother, Scott.
You are inspirations in the world of construction
and the beauty of life.
**—BRJ**

# IT'S TIME TO START!

There's work to do
at the new construction site!

To build a structure tall and strong,
machines will work
with all their
MIGHT!

# EXCAVATOR

rolls in slowly.
Without **WHEELS**
it moves on **TRACKS**.

ARM

BUCKET

CLICKETY-
**CLICK!**
It pushes forward.

# BULLDOZER

moves the mounds of dirt.
Its **METAL PLATE**
is **SHARP** and **WIDE**!

ENGINE

CAB

LIFT CYLINDER

BLADE

TRACK CHAINS

# FRONT-END LOADER

scoops the dirt! Then

# DUMP TRUCK

takes it for a ride!

# SKID STEER

is a small machine that's **ROUGH** and **TOUGH** and **QUICK**!

BUCKET

LOADER

For any jobs in tighter spaces,

BUCKET CYLINDER

TIRE

# A **GRADER**

levels lumpy ground, to make it **SMOOTH** and **STRAIGHT**.

Because it drives on rugged land,
it needs **SIX WHEELS** to

# OPERATE!

# The **MOBILE CRANE**

will carry things on-site
from **HERE** to **THERE**.

**BUCKETS** filled with **CONCRETE** will go floating through the

# A **FORKLIFT** does some lifting, too!

## When **BEAMS** and **BARS** go **HIGH**.

OVERHEAD GUARD

STEERING WHEELS

DRIVE WHEELS

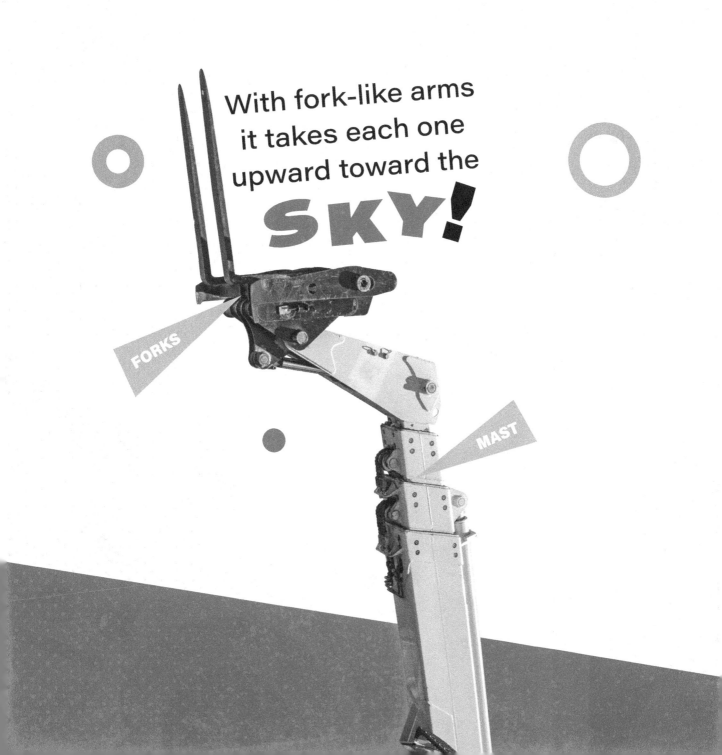

With fork-like arms
it takes each one
upward toward the
**SKY!**

It's time to move a pile of rocks.

# The **FRONT-END LOADER**

rumbles in.

# **DUMP TRUCK** waits until it's full, then unloads and returns again!

# A **ROLLER** rolls around the site,

## to compact earth and make it **STRONG**.

# VROOM! VROOM!

Machines will come and go.
Staying busy all day long.

Digging squares for concrete pads and columns now begins.

TRACK FRAME

ENGINE

BUCKET

CAB

COUNTERWEIGHT

The **TRACKHOE**'s arm is called a boom.

# ALARMS

sound when it's backing in!

BOOM

# CEMENT MIXER is driving in.

## It's fifty thousand pounds!

**OH NO**! Its wheels are sinking in!

# GLUB. GLUB.

It's stuck in squishy ground.

The **EXCAVATOR** comes to help.
**BULLDOZER** lends a big heave-ho!

Using thick and heavy chains,
they **LUG** and **TUG** and

# PULL
### and
# TOW!

The **MIXER** gets right back to work!

Its **DRUM** stirs up cement with care.

# A **FLATBED TRUCK**

will bring supplies with **LENGTH** and lots of **WEIGHT**.

Like **REBAR** for the **COLUMNS** that will stand up **TALL** and **STRAIGHT**.

# UP! UP! goes the structure.
# Now the **TOWER CRANE** is here.

It lifts a load. A **WHISTLE** blows!
To warn the workers—

PLEASE
STAY
CLEAR!

Level **ONE**, then Level **TWO**, then Level **THREE**
COMPLETE!

Made with **CABLES**, **BARS**, and **STEEL**, and **SUPER** strong **CONCRETE!**

# SWISH! SWISH!

## Go the FLOOR SWEEPERS,

doing their very best!

# POWER WASHERS

do their part to help clean up the mess!

# **LINES** are painted carefully, in **WHITE** and also **BLUE**.

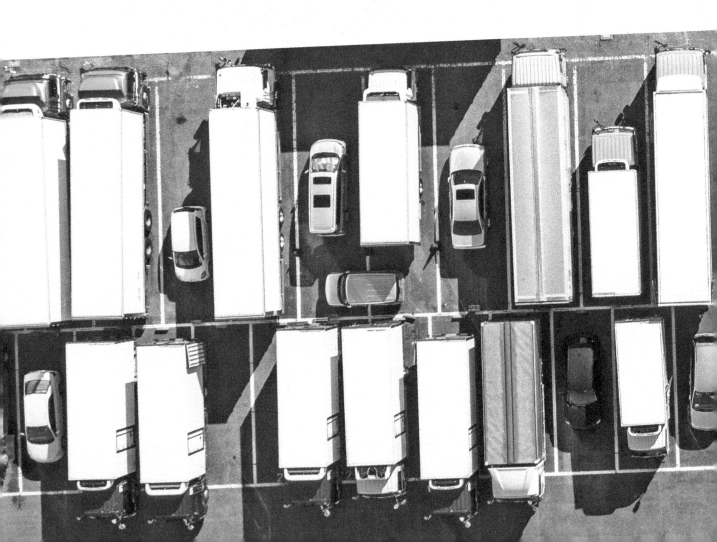

# Spaces made for **CARS** and **TRUCKS**— and **MOTORCYCLES**, too!

# The
# CONSTRUCTION
# MACHINES all love what they do!

They built a
**GARAGE** with
help from the crew!

# HERE THEY COME!

We're happy the construction is *FINALLY* done!

# BYE-BYE, CONSTRUCTION TRUCKS!

# ABOUT THE AUTHOR

Bonnie Rickner Jensen loves to write for children and believes every child on Earth holds a priceless purpose. She's a best-selling author who likes to be surrounded by picture books and people she loves, along with things from the places she's traveled. Born in Ohio, she now calls Florida home.